Sweet and Sour

Poetry & Prose

Suvarna

ISBN

Hardcase 979-8-89724-920-6
Paperback 979-8-89673-772-8

For my father,
my mother,
and my sister—
my heart, my roots, and my strength.

Introduction

Life is a mix of sweet and sour moments—the sweetness comes from those fleeting joys, love, and hope, while the sourness hits with heartbreak, loss, and those quiet nights that feel heavier than they should. This book was born out of both—the highs that make you feel unstoppable and the lows that leave you questioning everything.

So, why Sweet and Sour? If I'm being honest, it just feels kind of nice to say. Some of these poems dig deep, while others simply reflect the little thoughts, we all have—the ones that linger quietly in the background.

About a year ago, my life fell apart. I lost everything—the person I loved, my career, and for a time, I feared I might lose my mother too. One night, I found myself sitting alone in Dubai at midnight, with nowhere to go and barely enough money to make it to work the next day. I felt completely alone, and asking for help didn't seem like an option. But I had my laptop in my bag. So, I opened it and wrote my very first poem. That's how this journey began.

English isn't my first language, so if you notice a mistake or two, I hope you'll forgive me. My goal isn't perfection—it's connection. I wanted to share my story, raw and real, through these poems.

More than anything, I hope you'll find something here that resonates with you. While I can't fully capture your unique experiences, many of these poems are born from my own struggles, while others come from quiet moments of reflection on life.

Thank you for picking up this book. Even if you don't finish reading it, I'd be happy knowing it found a small place on your shelf or traveled with you in your bag.

She was strong for the longest time,
She wouldn't ask for help, even if she wanted to
Because getting help meant weakness,
But she was strong.
She wanted everything perfect for her kids,
So, she raised them on her own.
Then one fine day, she collapsed,
She forgot who she was,
She couldn't recognize her kids,
Everything became foreign to her.
It's like opening a book to read,
Yet, there aren't any words,
Just blank pages after pages,
There isn't any story,
Everything faded in the blink of an eye

When you feel hopeless,
I want you to pick up the habits
you loved as a child—
the ones you left behind
as you grew into adulthood.

Habits like painting or writing.
Even if you've forgotten
how to hold a brush,
I want you to pick it up.

Let the sound of brushstrokes
heal your soul.

Don't do it for attention
or with the pressure to create a masterpiece.
But remember—
some of the greatest works of art
were born from places of struggle,
where broken souls found their voice.

So, you'll never really know.

Just because it's dark
doesn't mean the sun doesn't exist.
There is always tomorrow,
a sunrise waiting to greet you.

And even if someday
you don't make it to tomorrow,
the light will always exist.

Don't let the pain change you.
Don't let it make you bitter and cold.
Because if you do, you become no different from the predators,
no different from those who planted agony in your chest.

So, please—never let them change you.

I don't trust people
who don't stand up for themselves.
I don't trust people
who are too terrified to protect their peace.
I don't trust people
who don't see their own worth.
I don't trust people
who don't love themselves.

And for the longest time,
I didn't trust myself either.
Because deep down, I knew—
how could I trust me
when I wasn't fair to myself?

But not anymore.

Falling in love for the first time—
nothing else you'll ever find feels just as warm and fine.

Your heart races, you feel a little nervous—
not in a bad way, but in a good way.

You smile at things that aren't even funny,
feeling foolish, yet weightless like honey.

You start admiring the moon and the sun,
and realize the best chapter has just begun.

It's awkward, exciting, a little terrifying,
yet you can't pretend; you have to admit—something's
changing.

First love stays, no matter how long,
even long after you've lost it all.

You were not my first love,
but you taught me what a partnership truly is.
We were a team,
learning to love and grow,
even when we both had so much to carry.

Although we couldn't last,
and maybe we weren't meant to make it to forever,
I will always be grateful for having you in my life.

Thank you for teaching me how to love better.
Thank you for showing me that love is more than
butterflies.
Thank you for reminding me that love is not possession.

Thank you.

Every time your eyes meet mine,
I want you to hold my gaze.

Reassure me a little more
that I am not the only one here,
feeling all of it.

Because if I am alone,
here with these emotions,
and you have never felt any of it,
the anguish would be unbearable.

What worse could happen to one
than falling in love,
all alone?

Lately, I have been revisiting the day we first met.
I still remember your sleepy face like it was yesterday.

I thought you were arrogant,
the way you treated me that day.
I would've never thought you'd be so vital for my
existence.

But you are important—
more than anyone or anything.

Now that I lost you,
I think I would never be happy without you.

Then again, what I think is not my future.
What's in store for me has nothing to do with my
thoughts.

So, I guess I'm okay to feel lost without you,
because I'll find myself again no matter what.

We stopped talking about it
like all of it was unreal,
something that never happened,
something we might have made up in our minds.
We stopped talking about it,
hoping we might not feel the same tomorrow,
hoping our memories together would fade with time
because time doesn't stop for anyone—
it goes on and on.
But you see, time wouldn't change anything,
yet it would force us to change ourselves.
So, we stopped talking about it
because we knew we'd have to change,
irrespective of what we felt.

You told me you don't love me anymore.
Though I wanted to confirm through your words,
I was not surprised.

I could see it in your eyes—
that I am not in your constellation anymore.
In your soul, something was dead for me.

I wanted to ask you:
Was it so easy?
Unloving me as if it was nothing.

It aches my heart, the thought of forgetting you.
So, every night I go to bed thinking:
Am I that easy to unlove?

The hardest part was not letting you go,
because I pictured a life with you.
I fantasized about myself in it.

Now that it's finally time to let go of you,
I have to let go of myself too.

The version of me I wanted to become felt absurd.
I had to forget about it.
I had to create another version of me.

I had to let go of you.
At the same time,
it was time to let go of the version of me
that wanted to create a life together.

I guess I was just afraid to lose myself.

I thought I could pull you out of darkness.
After all, darkness was not an unfamiliar place to me.
I ended up realizing I was just overestimating my abilities,
Risking you while I was drowning into an unknown chasm.

It's not true—I was loved.
That's why I stayed for so long.
I thought being loved was enough,
so I settled for it.

It's not right.
I deserved to be respected, supported, desired, and
understood.
Love was never enough!

I wanted you to hold me,
but you had better plans with someone else—
someone who isn't me.

I tried to make sense of it,
like all of it was a movie with an ending,
an ending that can be sad or happy.

At least I could try to rewrite our story,
but no amount of talent, effort, or love favored me.

I couldn't make you feel a thing.
It's heart-wrenching how I feel everything
while you feel nothing.

I thought that losing you would mean losing everything,
but it wasn't true.

Everything stayed the same—
my feelings and my longing for you.

The sole purpose of these eyes
was to see you until my last breath.

But when I lost you, everything remained the same—
except I lost myself.

Moving on from you felt like
leaving a part of me behind with you.
Gladly, I took a part of you as well.

However, I am well aware
these parts we shared
have already expired—
just a version of you and me
that no longer exists.

So, it's happening.
You are watching them lose interest in you.

One minute, you are special to them.
Now, you watch them drift away,
little by little.

You sit there, powerless—
a helpless creature, unable to stop them,
unable to change anything.

All you can do is watch them fade away,
like you were just a name on a paper,
no longer belonging to that page,
even if you wish to be in it.

I took a shower,
thinking of erasing you from my skin.

I rubbed all over me again and again.
No matter how hard I rubbed,
I kept feeling your touch.

I took another shower, thinking this time
I will wash you away.

I tried until my skin turned red.
Then I remembered—
you used to be amazed seeing my red skin.

Though I wanted to wash you away,
I ended up feeling you everywhere.

It would have been easier
if I could erase you with a shower.

You never had to fight for me.
Perhaps that was the biggest turn-off for you.

I was available, ready to embrace you at any time,
because you were my love.

But you were addicted to the idea of loving
someone who abuses you,
who treats you like an object.

But, darling, you've become that monster too.
And I became you—
someone addicted to the idea of chasing,
fighting, and screaming to earn your love.

It's sad how you've become my muse,
an inspiration to write more and more.

You are exactly what I can't have,
but I do love you!

You see, we don't really need a reason to love someone.
We love whoever we love.

I could think of 100 reasons not to love you,
yet I can't really stop myself from it.

I am just a helpless creature when it comes to you.

Those were your favorite flowers—
The ones you got me while waiting for me at the airport.
They were your favorite,
But somehow, they became mine.

Evening walks,
Stopping for coffee at your favorite café—
That became my favorite too.

Eating popcorn while watching Netflix...
I never even liked popcorn.
But you preferred it,
And who was I to deny you?

Now, you've found someone else—
Someone to share all your favorite things with.
And me?
I'm not even sure if I have favorites anymore.

Life feels like walking on a treadmill—
I am walking and walking,
yet ending up exactly where I started.

It sickens me, makes me wonder:
Will it always stay the same?
Will I ever break free from this chain?

But what is it that I am seeking?
In truth, I am unsure.

Yet walking the same path over and over,
and reaching no destination,
fills me with this strange sensation in my stomach.

I am sorry, I couldn't let you in—
not that I didn't want to, because I did.
I wanted you the very moment we met.

If I am being honest,
I needed you more than you needed me.

I am sorry, I couldn't let you in,
because I was terrified of seeing myself in your eyes.
Your eyes were speaking more than a million things all
at once,
desperately seeking company,
just the way I've been secretly seeking all this time.

I am sorry, I couldn't let you in—
not that I did not want love.
I wanted nothing more than that.

But when I looked at you, all I could see was myself,
and that scared me.

I am sorry, I couldn't let you in.

Heart
the little part of me beating,
Just to remind me I'm alive all the time.
I wonder how much it can take,
Cause I can feel it in my chest.
It's been enduring this weight.
Poor little heart,
how do I get to thank you?
You're the only one who hasn't given up on me yet.

She isn't a poet.
She couldn't rhyme even if she wanted to.
She used the F-word a lot—
A lot more than people around her would.

*F*ck when she's happy,*
*F**ck when she's sad,
F**ck when she's anxious,*
*F**ck when she's excited,
F*ck when she's pleasured.

She shows up for people—
A lot more than others would,
Even when they don't acknowledge her.

Was it because she grew up
With low self-esteem?
Or because she knows too well
How it feels to be lonely?

It took forever to understand
How beautiful it is to be on my own—
My little, peaceful paradise.

I make mistakes all the time.
I repeat them too.
But the worst of it all
Was making you cry on your birthday—
The day I realized you deserved better.
You deserved someone who makes you feel special,
Someone who stands next to you.
Not me.
Not someone who's the reason for the tears on your
cheeks.

So, I did the only thing I could do:
I released you.
I freed you.
Because I loved you—and always will—from this distance.

I love you
Like I love the moon, the sun, and the stars,
Although the moon, the sun, and the stars will never
acknowledge me.

Sometimes, I feel empty,
and I don't know
if I am missing the parts of you,
or the parts of me
that existed with you.

Nothing feels right when home doesn't feel like home.
Nothing is worse than feeling lonely in a crowded room.

Nothing is harder than thinking of you
while lying next to someone else.

Nothing is more terrible than the flames
still burning for you in my chest,
even though you no longer belong to me.

Nothing is as painful as realizing
I say "sorry" more than I should
just to keep you in my life.

Why does everything seem right when it isn't?

You said I was like rain in your life,
bringing warmth to the dryness you carried.

Trust me, I am flattered by what you said,
but both of us forgot the fact—
too much rain could also lead to a flood,
and people could drown in it.

Although I was happy to be the rain in your life,
the earth couldn't contain the overflowing water.
It led to a flood,
leaving you to drown without a grip.

I don't write about you anymore.
In fact, I don't even feel anything the way I used to.

Although it's a relief,
I wonder:
What if I became cold—
cold enough to feel nothing at all
when I should be mourning you,
when I should be crying over you?

Forgetting that I have been crying my eyes out
all this time.

I finally see everything clearly,
stopped sugarcoating,
stopped thinking about a dead memory in my head—
again, and again.

It's over. I am not sad anymore,
and that is okay,
isn't it ironic?

I said I don't write about you,
yet I am writing about you now
when I could be doing a million other things.

I had overflowing love
That you refused to accept.
I tried to find places and people to drop it,
But all of it that I gave away
Ended up in the trash—
Unrecognized,
Unappreciated.

In the end,
I had to give it to myself.

Everything you seek,
The answers, the light, the peace—
It's all within you.

I didn't know the depth of my love for you
until I lost you.

The grief that I carried in my chest for a decade
was an honest reflection of the joy I once felt.

I thought it would last forever.
Perhaps that's why I couldn't prepare myself
for this anguish.

For my whole life, I dreamt of freedom—
the liberation from people, places, and expectations.

I even considered freedom as my ultimate purpose.
That's how I knew you were special.

For the first time, I craved to be in a cage,
as long as you were in it with me.

I needed nothing more.
It was liberating to be locked up with you—
you and me,
having you by my side,
waking up next to you,
watching you grow older.

There is nothing more liberating in life
than being locked up with you in a cage.

We are told not to go out at night
so that we can protect our bodies,
but our sons deserve to be out,
having fun at their party.

Daughters are not allowed to work late
'cause they are not safe in the dark.

Was it darkness, though,
the problem?

"Stay home, and you'll be safe"—
but was she safe at home?
Was she safe when she was surrounded by the predator?

She was never told that it could be her own father,
brother, uncle—
and the list goes on and on.

How can she protect herself when she wasn't told
that it wasn't the darkness lurking outside?

It's those faces she might be trusting.
It wasn't the darkness;
darkness was never the problem.

You are a woman—
Keep your voice down.
You are a woman—
Don't wear anything that might provoke men.
You are a woman—
Don't go out at night.
You are a woman—
Don't smile; it could be seen as a sign.
You are a woman—
Don't be the center of attention.
You are a woman—
Don't exist.

I wonder why this world is unfair.
The rich become richer,
the poor become poorer.

If you are abused, then it's your fault—
'cause you let them abuse you.
Why did you let them?
And why are you complaining now?
Why can't you keep it to yourself?
Is it fun playing the victim?

I want these pointless noises to stop,
yet I know they won't.

How can one cope with these noises?
How can one cope when it's hard to live with oneself?
When everyone blames you for your own pain,
how can you cope?

When life threw lemons,
they said, "Make lemonade."
Easier said than done—
for her, life only threw stones.

She didn't know what to do
with the weight of those stones.
For a fleeting moment,
she thought of throwing them back—
recklessly.
But she didn't.
That, too, felt exhausting.

Instead, she stacked them,
one by one,
building a wall around herself.
Each stone made it stronger,
solid enough to protect her.
Inside, it was quiet,
peaceful… or so she thought.

Until the darkness settled in.
And she wondered:
Would it have been better
if life had thrown lemons instead of stones?

The pain might have been lighter,
easier to swallow.
It's awful to drink lemonade too often—
but at least it wouldn't be so dark inside.

Choosing the best for someone isn't love.
Telling someone to do things the "right" way isn't love.
Keeping someone tied to you isn't love.

Love is liberating.
Love is understanding that your beloved has their own
self—
Their own feelings,
Their own choices,
And most importantly, an identity that exists beyond you.

Love is standing by their side,
Wanting their happiness,
And respecting their choices,
Even if one day, their choice is to grow away from you.

40°C temperature.
I saw a man sweeping the glass of a tall building—
he was hanging on a rope,
that rope preventing him from falling.

For a minute, I thought to myself:
was this his dream?

Perhaps, he dreamt of becoming an artist,
but ended up sweeping the glass of a skyscraper.

If you look closer, there's art in it too—
and risk as well.
But...
is he content?

Perhaps, he is.
What if he had a dream
that shattered right in front of him?
What if he carried responsibilities on his shoulders,
forcing him to give up on those dreams?
What if hanging on a rope
isn't his dream?

What if?

Then I asked myself:
Am I worried about him
or myself?

Am I living my dream?

What if
money will never be enough?
What if
a decent job will never be fulfilling?
What if,
after retirement, there's no time left to live?
What if,
even after all the effort,
sweeping will never become an art?

And what if,
in the end,
we realize that we spent our lives chasing something
that was never truly ours to begin with?

In the last ten years, Earth has been spinning—
three thousand six hundred fifty-two times.
An endless journey, seeking something,
yet reaching nowhere.

Do planets long for something, too,
like I longed for you?

Circling the Sun, a destined journey,
each orbit a hope, yet no destination.
Perhaps to arrive would be destruction,
for even the planet, in its longing,
cannot handle the Sun's fierce, intense heat—
though it feels the warmth from afar,
a yearning just to be yearned.

Perhaps the Sun is meant to protect Earth
and other cosmic objects from afar.

I wonder if the Sun would also possibly long to belong,
yet bound to stand alone, untouchable,
cursed by its own blessings and powers.

Accepting this distance as the only truth,
longing for connection, yet forever in solitude.

The door closed in my face,
Darkness filled my eyes,
Fear wrapped itself around me,
And most of all—
Hopelessness.

But I found the light within.
It took a while,
Yet I always find it,
No matter how the darkness grips me,
No matter how it returns each time.

You don't need anyone's permission
To embrace your truth,
To stand tall in your own skin,
To be unapologetically you.

Although you don't see it,
There are always stars
Shining in your eyes.
You were born with them.
I wish you could see the beauty
You carry within.

It's a pity you don't see it for yourself.
Even when people tell you,
You brush it off,
As if you've convinced yourself
That you are not beautiful.

~you are enchanting

Love is a cure,
but it can be a deadly disease too—
one that won't end you soon
but will let you suffer,
like glass breaking into thousands of pieces
with no way to put it back together.

You still believe that love is the cure,
that your beloved will wipe all the pain away.
So, waiting feels like the only way—
but what if you're waiting just to let time fly?

Perhaps, love is a cure,
and you are waiting for your beloved.
But what if love is you?
What if you need to wipe the pain on your own?

That is love too—
it has always been with you,
waiting for you to acknowledge it.

I love my coffee cup.
I always keep it by my side,
As if it is a treasure.
Sometimes, I just imagine, what if?
What if it breaks?
It could shatter into small little pieces on the floor.
Then the thought that I could pick up all those pieces
And glue them back together gives me hope.
What a relief, yet I feel restless.
Perhaps gluing it back together makes it even more beautiful,
Artistic!
but not the same.

Sometimes, I wish I could understand her,
but I don't.

No matter how hard I try to put myself into her shoes,
I just can't fit in.

Just the way she doesn't understand me,
I think there is beauty in it too.

Being mysterious to each other will only make us crave
more.
We live trying to learn something we are incapable of
knowing.

She woke to the emptiness,
Yet carried hope in her chest.
Day and night,
She told herself,
"The world will turn around."

So, she did the only thing she could—
Woke up to the emptiness,
Holding tightly
To the hope in her chest.

I thought the world ended that night—
But it didn't.
I thought I would suffocate—
But I didn't.

There was a time I believed
Things would never change—
But they did.
I thought I'd never move on—
But I have.

Now I know, no matter how hard life gets,
Even if I burn to ashes,
There will come a time
To rise again.

From the ashes,
I will rise.

I woke up this morning feeling grumpy.
Admitting it would make me angry.

But there is no perfect way of living,
other than feeling
what I feel.

So,
I admitted it.

But then they asked me why—
the reason for my feelings—
as if I'm not allowed to feel anything
without conditions.

I tried to find the root of it all,
just to end up nowhere.

I guess
I just woke up this morning feeling grumpy.

This disease called boredom is killing me slowly.
It's not that I have free time.

In fact, I am pretty occupied with my full-time work,
paying bills,
and doing dishes.

I hardly get time even to do these chores sometimes.
To be honest, I haven't talked to my mother
or my sister
for a long time.

I feel distant,
yet I yearn for something unknown.

I am walking closer to my death like anyone else,
which makes me wonder:
after all, what is my purpose?

Some say it is to believe what they believe,
and I realize—
believing would permanently close the doors of my
investigations.

I want to live for the endless possibilities.
However, I can't hide the fact that I am bored.

The routine,
bills,
dishes,
my own thoughts—
everything feels like nothing.

Empty...

I hope we could meet
In another universe,
Where we both meet halfway,
Where we don't press pause—unfinished.

I hope in another universe,
We'll play our movie till the end.
I'm not sure if there's another universe,
But if there is,
I promise to love you in every single one—
Even if you decide to press pause,
Even if you're unwilling
To let it play till the end.

To love is to let go.
It took me forever to learn that.
Perhaps that's why I found reasons to keep you in my
life.
I lived every second trying to find ways to tie your
hands,
keeping you to myself—
to a point where you saw me as a monster,
a monster who was not ready to let you go.

It's funny how I reminisce the past—
a fragile collection of memories,
carefully crafted with you,
once wrapped with happiness.

Now, they're nothing but pain—
a thorned bouquet pressed against my chest,
cutting not deep enough to end,
an unexplainable misery.

All you need is space—
at least, that's what you say.

But it's really hard—
waiting as seconds turn to minutes,
minutes to hours, hours to days,
days to weeks, weeks to even months.

The worst part of it all?
We don't even know how long this will last.

I wonder—
is this your way of pushing me away?
Is this your way of ending things with me?
Is this your way of leaving me behind?
Is this your way of abandoning me?

Even when I try to stop my racing mind,
I can't comprehend the fact that you need space from me.
I can't live with your ghost.

The space between us doesn't seem to fade;
it grows with every passing second.
I feel deserted and abandoned.

She loved you fearlessly,
Though you never loved her the same.
You treated her like an option,
While she made you, her choice.

She gave you chance after chance,
And all you did was break her heart.
You disrespected her,
Yet she stood by your side,
Even when you were never there for her.

She deserved the world,
But you were homeless.

Enough is enough.
She is done being a lovesick girl.
She stands on her own now,
Rooted, strong, and steady.

She carries the world within her,
And no longer will your inability to love
Stop her from being the most loving,
The most giving person she is.

No longer will she let you
Change her heart.

She is fearless.
She is whole.
She is enough.

Most of all,
She deserves the world.

I am a wanderer locked in a cage,
all of me consumed by rage.

Yet I can't break these chains—
I try to calm my racing brain,
hoping someday things will change,
but I can feel my body age.

Tell me, is it worth the breaking
when the clock is steadily ticking?

I'm unsure what lies beyond—
will I find another cage, or be gone?

Once I break down this wall,
will I only find another cage,
or a chance to escape it all?

Sometimes, I don't know if I should cry,
because tears won't change anything.
Instead, they pull me deeper into a pit of pain,
reminding me of my darkest days—
as if I'm stuck in a room without lights.

I find myself on my knees, choking,
grasping for breath,
yet hope feels so far away.

I wish I could be carefree,
but I feel everything just a little too deeply.
They say crying isn't a sign of weakness,
but there's that look in their eyes
when they see the tears in mine.

I don't want their pity,
so I'd rather keep it to myself—
sit alone in the darkness,
fighting my own demons.

I knew—
all along,
we were never meant to last.

I knew you would never stay forever.
We were a fleeting story,
written in borrowed time.

Yet still, I hoped—
for the impossible,
for you to choose love,
to choose us.

But some stories
are only meant to be
a fleeting joy,
a spark that fades.

You thought I was weak.
My emotions were unfamiliar to someone like you,
So you concluded I was weak.

But I felt the same about you—
You, who were overwhelmed by emotions,
Who built walls instead of bridges.

It's a pity—
You won't even sympathize.
I thought you were weak to feel.
Perhaps I was weak to think you were weak,
Because there is always hope—
You can sympathize if you let yourself.

There you go,
breaking down my world
right before my eyes.

So, you were just another lesson—
a lesson I had to learn,
and let go of.

But I still don't understand
how you became a part of my lungs,
because we were two different people.

Yet, somehow,
I forgot how to breathe
when you left me behind.

In the generation of one-night stands,
I asked myself:

"But what is, after all, one night?
A short space, especially when the darkness flies so soon,
and so soon the sun will rise.
What then?
Is it just a distraction from reality,
or a coping mechanism?"

They say, "Don't love until it's permanent,"
but how do I love with conditions?
How do I stop my heart
when it beats for someone on its own?

If you look closer, life is absurd.
If that is true, what is the point of living?

Some say we must live to love and to be loved.
I thought that was absurd too—until you.

I started seeing the stars and skies in your eyes.
Oh God! Your eyes!!!

Finally, all those movies, books, and poems felt real.
I saw the universe without even opening my eyes.

You took me to another realm,
where you and I are everything,
where I wanted nothing more than us—
just us.

The word *absurd* no longer existed.
I found the definition of life with you in it

She pulls me into her arms,
creating a space I never had.
Her warmth, the greatest gift—
one I never knew existed.

She is the shoulder I cry on,
not the shush that silences my pain,
but the embrace that lets me feel,
and the warmth that lets me heal.

I have found love once.
Then I lost it.

It's like I am on top of the tallest building in the world,
and I ended up losing my grip—
falling down to the concrete floor,
bleeding with broken bones,
laying down wide awake.

And I don't want to die.

I feel the pain in every inch.
In fact, I want to feel more of it,
because that pain is the only link
to the love I had once.

I Don't Understand

I still don't understand How I provoke you.
Although you don't know me,
You haven't seen my soul,
Yet my existence somehow
Manages to provoke you.

I don't understand.
Why my being, my quiet breath,
Stirs something bitter in you.

Why do you care so much?
Why spend your precious time
To make others feel worse about themselves,
To plant doubt in their chest?

Is the fire you throw at others
Just the ash of what burns within you?

I don't understand.
And maybe, I never will.

Every time you say,
"I'm fine,"
with that smile on your face,
I can't help but think—
you deserve an Oscar.

She is not a mopey person,
yet she feels everything a little too much—
too much, like she can feel a thump on her chest,
to a point where she wishes she did not have a heart
or a body.

She is not a mopey person,
yet she is overwhelmed most of the time.

Most of the time
is another way of saying
all of the time.

She is not a mopey person.

I didn't love you because you are perfect.
I remember you saying there was no reason for me to
love you.

And it's true—
you did literally nothing to make me fall for you.

In fact, I'm not blinded.
I see your weaknesses.
I see the wrinkles and dots on your face.
I see how imperfect you are, both inside and out.

Isn't it funny?
All of your imperfections are just perfect to me.

You are exactly what I want
out of a billion beautiful people.

They say love is a drug,
and I think they're right.
It hits like a high,
keeps me up all night.

Dopamine rushes,
I'm smiling too wide.
But when you're not here,
it feels empty inside.

I crave your touch,
your voice, your time.
Each word you say
feels like a rhyme.

They call it chemistry,
the science of the heart.
But it's more than that—
it tears me apart.

I'm restless, I'm hooked,
can't seem to let go.
Am I addicted to love?
I think I know.

It's the craving, the longing,
the rush, the despair.
A cycle of joy
and pain I can't bear.

Love is an addiction,
and I'm lovesick, it's true.
But the worst of it all—
I'm addicted to you.

I had a theory when I was growing up:
Every time it rained,
I thought it was because the sky was sad.

The sky, shedding teardrops through the rain—
Every drop that touched the ground
A symbol of agony.

I used to believe,
Even the sky wasn't exempt
From the weight of misery.

I know how it feels to love someone deeply,
yet they don't want your love.

No matter how much you care,
how long you'd wait for them—
like a flower withering in shadow,
how many sleepless nights you've spent
praying they'd bloom in your light,
how hard you try to make them happy—
they don't want it.

They don't want your love.

I'm not saying it's their fault,
but you reach a point where your heart
becomes a flame that burns without warmth.

All you know about love becomes pain.

They say, "Don't regret your actions,"
but sometimes I can't help myself from regretting.

Yet, I say it out loud:
"I do not regret,"
although I feel slighted inside.

At least I can hide,
keep a wise smile,
hoping that faking would become reality—
if you fake it enough
and believe in your lie.

A writer's attempt
to make a lie the truth.

There are times when people have been unkind to me,
but they couldn't be worse than the voices inside me,
reminding me, over and over, that I'm not worthy,
that I don't belong.

I try to fight it, but
fighting this voice isn't easy—
especially when I can't tell which part of me is speaking.

Is it a friend in disguise,
or an enemy tearing me apart?

Some days, the voice wins.
Some days, there's a tiny voice reminding me that I'm enough—
like a child yelling in a crowded room.

It's funny how I wake up in the morning,
Forgetting you're not lying next to me.
The emptiness fools me for a moment,
Until reality hits me with the cold side of the bed.

You said you don't care,
but your eyes say otherwise.

Your eyes are filled with love, care, and concern.
There is so much in you that you gave to this world
willingly,
and you claim not to expect anything in return.

Yet you gaze at each pair of eyes you meet so deeply,
hoping to find a piece of you.

You shrug it off, like nothing can break you,
yet you spend midnights fighting with those little noises
in your head.

I hope you realize the piece you've been searching for is
within you.
I hope you realize people talk more about themselves
than others.
I hope someday, you fiercely protect yourself enough
to admit that you do care.

I'm starting to move on.
It doesn't mean I think you are an awful person.
In fact, I am not trying to unlove you.

It doesn't mean I'm not hurting.
I'm in more pain than ever.
But I decided to sit with it.
Feel it.
Allow it to break me into pieces.
Explore every layer of it.

Because I enjoyed every second when you loved me.
And all I am left with is this pain—
not your love.

So, I'm going to face it
until it makes me feel nothing.

I Realized

Living alone can be lonely,
Yet the taste of solitude is heavenly—
A flavor I never knew existed.

Slowly, I stopped explaining,
Stopped seeking validation.
I owe you nothing to be me,
To live authentically,
To breathe freely.

The weight of fitting in—
It pressed on my chest for so long,
But not anymore.

Now, I see the peace within me,
The quiet beauty in sipping coffee,
Alone, all by myself.

Opposites attract,
But that's not entirely true.
I found pieces of me in your eyes,
Pieces I didn't know were missing.

The more time I spent with you,
The more I realized—
We are the same,
Though from the outside,
We appear so different.

I realized now—
you fell out of love with yourself
because I was in your life.

I fell in love with myself
because you were in mine.

Yet I'm still unsure who was wrong.
Was it me or you?
Should we blame something else?
Or maybe, none of us was wrong at all

Loving you felt like being locked in an apartment with a
serial killer—
a place that was my entire world.

A kitchen,
a bedroom,
a bathroom that flushed away the evidence of your
victims,
and a window that was my only glimpse of freedom.

You were cruel.
You could break my body,
rip apart my soul
as easily as you pleased.

Yet, you gave me glimpses of hope—
tiny sparks of happiness,
making me believe
that if I endured a little longer,
I could change you.
I could make you human,
make you normal,
make you love.

But hope was a weapon in your hands,
a tool to keep me wrapped around you.
Every time you shattered me,
you put me back together,
only to break me again.

I knew—
I knew I couldn't change a monster.
But you were the only warmth I had,
and even your cruel arms felt like home.

So I clung to you,
holding tightly, desperately,
even as your embrace
ached to tighten around my throat.

She packed her bags—
ready to step into a new life,
with new people,
a new place to call home.

A rice cooker, a frying pan, a coffee pot.
Four pairs of clothes—just enough to survive.
She was ready to say goodbye.

She would live in a city,
embrace new experiences,
find new faces to fill her days.

And though it was a relief,
she couldn't escape herself.
She was trapped—
trapped in her own body,
a silent prison she carried everywhere.

Even as she left everything behind,
she realized some things
could never be left behind.

Taking a sip from a cup of tea
that cost no more than 10 rupees,
standing on the sidewalk,
watching the world's symphonies—
it taught me more about life
than any degrees.

Humans inhale oxygen
and exhale carbon dioxide—
to live,
we need the oxygen in the air.

But that night,
you were too close,
so close that I breathed in
the carbon dioxide you exhaled.

And for the very first time,
I felt alive.
My whole life,
oxygen couldn't make me feel—
couldn't make me feel like I was truly living.

But your carbon dioxide did.

Her mother's eyes never softened,
her touch, always distant.
Alone, she grew—
her shadow her only companion.

She wandered into the arms of others,
giving pieces of her heart,
hoping they would cherish them.

But they left her on seen.
No explanations, no closure—
just the quiet reminder:
she was a fleeting season,
destined to fade away.

Each goodbye carved deeper into her soul,
solidifying her biggest fear:
she was unlovable,
a storm waiting for someone
who'd never come.

I hate the way I look at myself in the mirror,
just to remember the very moment
you held my gaze—
like I was everything you ever needed to see.

The rest of the world
blurred,
faded
into insignificance.

And now, I hate to think of it,
because I don't know anymore—
was it real?

Did I delude myself,
or did you truly see me
the way I thought you did?

I don't know.
I thought I knew,
but not anymore.

I saw him lying there, his skin turned blue.
Cold, heavy, lifeless.
It felt like stone.

He was there, but not really him.
Not the person I knew.
Something in me just knew.

I screamed.
I screamed so loud,
hoping he'd hear me from wherever he was,
hoping maybe my voice could reach him, pull him back.

But the truth hit me.
The person lying there...
It wasn't him.
It wasn't him.
I could feel it in my bones.

I have been searching for myself.
Don't get me wrong—I am right here, writing this piece.
But not the version I've been looking for.
The version that was naive, that found joy in little
things.
The version that could look up to him,
that always had his back,
that was seen by him.

I have been searching for myself,
but that version is nowhere to be found.
Because that version burned into ashes—with him.

Perhaps I need to find a version of myself
that never existed before.
One that never had him in the first place.

What I've been looking for could never be found.
I had to invent myself all over again.

That morning, you were doing your laundry.
The last time I saw you,
you were doing your laundry—avoiding my eyes.

I see now,
it wasn't shame about liking me.
It wasn't disgust.
You were grappling with emotions you weren't ready to
face.

And I understand.
I've been there too.

I used to break myself down,
but now I'm learning to rebuild.
I was ready to admit how I felt,
even if I didn't always value myself.

But today,
I see my worth,
and I know that love—true love—starts with me.

What we couldn't admit then,
I embrace now:

I thought we were soulmates.
Why else would my heart race,
like it's about to throw up, every time?

Not that I wanted it to react that way.
A thousand things on my mind,
a million words ready to spill—
but I end up saying nothing.

That was the intensity I felt when you were near.
I thought all of this meant something,
that these were the signs of finding a soulmate.

Like how nothing else matters
when I meet your eyes,
or how, when we're together,
the rest of the world fades into nothing—
and we become everything.

It's been a decade.
I told myself I've moved on.
I even forgot your last birthday.

I'm no longer sure of your height.
Maybe you're taller,
your hair shorter,
your face thinner.

I can't predict from your profile picture,
but I remember your dark eyes—
deep as galaxies.
I remember the curve of your lips when you smile,
how you'd smile at my stupidity,
at my clumsiness.

Although I've moved on,
I still search for your eyes
when I meet someone new—
maybe I could find a piece of you in them.

You were never mine;
I was never yours.

You never wanted my love,
but I loved you anyway.
You never needed me,
but I stayed in your orbit,
hoping you would feel what I felt.
But you never did.

Sometimes I pity you for not feeling it,
because it was magical—
something out of space and time,
beyond human imagination,
something I cannot put into words.

I pity you for not feeling it,
but I felt it anyway—
though it was quite lonely
here all by myself.

I saw her skin shrinking,
color dimming,
memory fading.

Piece by piece,
she was losing herself.

I didn't know what was worse—
having her beside me,
with none of her left,
or watching
life slip away.

I've always admired you—
your brilliance, your sharp mind,
the way you unravel the world with such ease.

Yet somehow, you never understood me.
You couldn't see my loud, raw heart,
beating recklessly, only for you.

You said goodbye.
All you wanted was an escape,
but all I needed was for you to stay.

And then I remembered—
the sun doesn't wait for me to set.
No matter how much I wish to hold on to the dawn,
it doesn't ask for my permission to leave.

I was sipping coffee at a café,
lost in my thoughts,
contemplating life.

That's when I noticed a family.
I've always adored watching families spend time
together—
it warms my heart.
But that day, my perspective shifted.

The father sat there,
consumed by his own world.
The mother struggled to feed their little boy,
who was too engrossed in a YouTube video to notice her.

They were a family—
together, yet so profoundly disconnected.

In that moment,
they made me realize something unexpected:
the true value of my solitude.

They say, when you know, you know.
But I don't know.
Not anymore.

I knew when I was seventeen.
I was so sure of you.
But now I'm twenty-seven,
and I don't know.

It's heartbreaking, isn't it?
How I could feel so certain back then,
only for the world to rip us apart,
like we were never meant to be.

You and I—
we had to be terrified
just to feel something real,
to have feelings of our own.

They say, when you know, you know.
But they decided for me.
They silenced what I knew
when I was sure of you.

Maybe someday I'll know again.
Maybe I'll find that certainty.
But I'm scared—
scared they'll take it from me again.

We said we were friends,
yet there was something about our fingers intertwined,
something in the way we looked at each other—
lingering, unspoken, undeniable.

We said we were friends,
but we lived every second chasing excuses
to touch, to feel, to stay near.

Friends don't hold each other's hands
like their very existence depends on it.
Yet, we did.

We were friends,
but the way our breaths tangled in the silence,
the way our eyes lingered just a moment too long—
friends don't do that, do they?

We said we were friends,
yet every second was a prayer,
hoping one day we'd find the courage
to admit we were so much more
than just friends.

When I said
we belong together forever,
I meant it.
Or maybe I just wanted it—
wanted you in my life,
where I could never grow tired of you.

Even if your smile stayed the same,
I could live in the curiosity
of how you'd grow,
of how we'd grow—
watching us age,
to the point where walking became a struggle.
But still,
we'd hold each other—
wouldn't we?

I wanted all of this,
but fate had other plans for you.
And yet, you stayed with me,
in the words I write—
words that may linger
long after I'm gone,
keeping you here,
forever.

I don't believe in heaven,
but if we were still together,
I might have believed
it was heavenly.

I don't believe in the supernatural,
but when you were near,
I felt invisible strings—
tying us,
binding us,
together.

I wanted to disappear
when I was seventeen.
The moment I tasted you,
I wanted to be gone.

Not because you tasted like hell,
but because you felt too good.
Too good—
something I'd never known,
something that shook the ground beneath my soul.

I wanted to be gone,
not from you, but from myself.
Terrified,
thinking you might have tasted hell in me.

Why else would you walk away,
after all that we had been?
You left me in silence,
with nothing
but the ache to disappear.

She loved him,
but he wanted her to prove her love—
to prove it by leaving him,
by releasing him.

He was her everything.
She carried his children,
she dreamed of a life with him.
But he wanted her to show her love
by setting him free.

You said,
"If we're meant to be together, we will be.
No one can rip us apart.
All we need is patience—
to wait,
to wait for our reunion."

And though it was devastating,
I held on to hope.

But I never saw you make an effort—
to see me,
to be with me,
to talk to me.

You said,
"If we're meant to be together, we will be."
I guess you always knew
we were never meant to be.

You never looked back,
but I often think about you.
Not in the way I used to,
yet you return to me
in the quiet moments of the night,
when I'm in bed, trying to sleep,
when the sky turns darker.

I can't help but wonder where you are.
I wanted to hate you,
hoped that hate could erase you away.
But hating you never worked—
it couldn't erase the memories of you.

You never looked back,
but I did.
I dissected what we had,
over and over,
trying to understand
how we lost something so real.

You were never perfect,
and I never asked you to be.
You weren't meant to—
you were you,
and that was enough for me.

I loved you
through the cracks,
through the chaos.

But you never loved me.
You said I wasn't perfect for you,
said we'd grow bored someday,
as if love needed perfection
to last.

But I was enough for me.
And one day,
I'll be enough for someone else.

I watched you burn into ashes.
At that very moment,
nothing around me made sense.
Everything felt absurd—
and still,
I watched you burn into ashes.

I want to be your lover,
to become the person
who brings warmth to your constellation,
who stands by your side,
never drifting apart
or playing hard to get.

I want to be your lover,
yet at times, I feel I'm only meant to write—
to write about love,
to write about being your lover,
or simply about wanting to be yours.

We are colorblind—
we live in black and white,
in dark and light,
in right and wrong.

Though we know,
don't we?
There are colors—infinite and untamed,
a kaleidoscope of possibilities,
each shade whispering a story,
a truth, a perspective.

We know, don't we?
Yet we choose not to believe
in anything more
than black and white.

The beauty of silence
in your solitude
often feels scary yet necessary—
a space to comprehend the world,
yourself,
and everything else,
especially while living in absurdity.

The little details—
the sound of a dog
barking next door,
a motorcycle passing by—
every little thing
pulls you back to yourself.

As a kid,
I used to ask myself,
What is love?
I tried to crack the code
by watching movies,
listening to music,
and reading poems.

I found countless definitions,
each crafted by artists in their own way.
But then I met you.

In that moment, I felt something—
something deep,
beyond my imagination,
beyond any definition.

I felt it.
I felt love—
so limitless,
it surpassed every definition
I had ever known,
combined

I dreamed of being yours,
but sadly,
not every dream
is meant to come true.

So, I made it possible—
what I once thought impossible.
I thought I'd choke to death
without you.

Indeed, it was difficult to breathe
at times when your absence
weighed heavier than air itself.

Yet, I learned to live.
I learned to pretend—
to act like hearing your name
didn't shake me to my core.
I mastered the art
of acting unbothered,
as if it didn't matter
that you moved on
with someone else.

And now,
I've learned to love you
from a distance,
something I once thought impossible.

I liked the pain you
inflicted on me
because it reminded me
that I am alive.

It made me feel the heart
in my chest beating,
even as it felt like choking.

I liked the pain you
inflicted on me,
because in the ache,
I found proof of life.

Don't let them silence you
or dictate the volume of your voice.
Don't let them shame you for being loud.

Waves don't quiet down.
Thunder doesn't apologize.
Volcanoes don't ask for permission to erupt.

Never regret standing up for yourself.

Ironically, I see it now—
how I've been lonely all along,
even when I was lying next to you.

Now, as I stand alone,
on my own,
I don't feel lonely at all.

It's quiet,
silence wrapping itself around me—
not empty, but full.
Peaceful.
Content.